THE
MUNCHY
MUNCHY
Cookbook
for Kids

FAMILIUS

Published by Familius LLC, www.familius.com

Familius books are available at special discounts for bulk purchases, whether
for sales promotions or for family or corporate use. For more information, contact
Familius Sales at 559-876-2170 or email orders@familius.com.

Library of Congress Cataloging-in-Publication Data
2019903663

Print ISBN 9781641701563
Ebook ISBN 9781641702119

Printed in China

Edited by Lacey Wulf, Sarah Echard, and Alison Strobel
Cover and book design by Pierre A. Lamielle and Derek George

10 9 8 7 6 5 4 3 2 1

First Edition

THE Munchy Munchy Cookbook

for Kids

ESSENTIAL SKILLS AND RECIPES
EVERY YOUNG CHEF SHOULD KNOW

Pierre A. Lamielle

table of contents

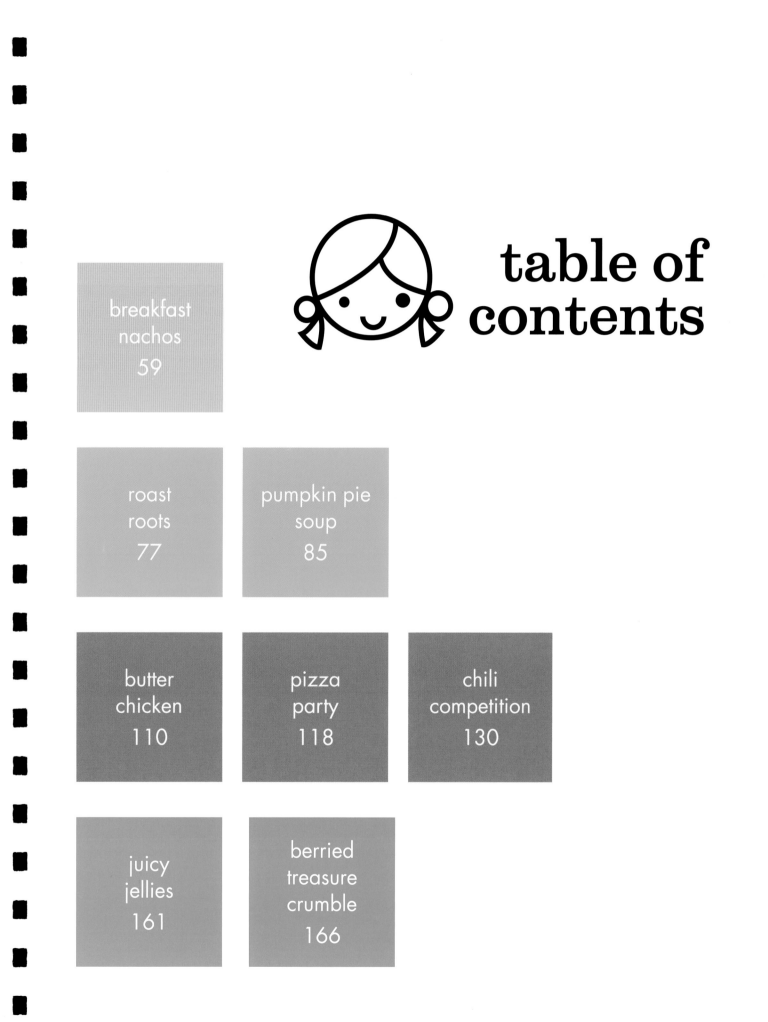

cooking is delicious,
but it can also be
dangerous

look for these warnings
with each recipe

sharp **hot** **germs**

and read the safety pages
to avoid getting cut, burned, or sick

sharp

hot

germs

SHARP THINGS CUT YOU,

how to hold a knife properly

GET A GRIP

Hold the handle with all fingers and thumb on the handle

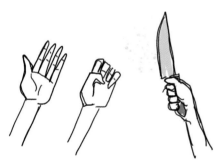

CURL YOUR FINGERS

Keep your fingertips curled under so your knuckles are closest to the knife

TUCK YOUR THUMB

Tuck your thumb in with your fingers, not out the side

how to move a knife properly

SLICE

Start slowly, use a sliding forward motion starting at the front of the knife and ending at the back of the knife when your knife contacts the board.

HINGE

With the point down on the cutting board, start with the handle up high and bring it down to the board.

SAW

This works best for a serrated knife with the little saw-like ridges. Simply slide the knife back and forth without pressing down.

AND YOU DON'T WANT THAT!

different kinds of knives

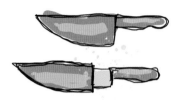

PARING KNIFE
Some paring knives come with a plastic protective cover for safety. Keep the cover on when you are not cutting.

CHEF KNIFE
A big knife that should be used with caution. Only use this knife if you are comfortable with sharp tools.

SERRATED KNIFE
A long knife with ridges that make it easy to use a sawing motion to cut difficult things like soft bread and tomatoes.

other sharp things

GRATERS AND ZESTERS
are very sharp and can really hurt your knuckles.

PEELER
With two little blades, this piece of equipment is more dangerous than it looks.

ASSORTED EQUIPMENT
Food processors and blenders all have sharp blades to cut, chop, and blend food.

if you get cut

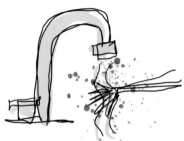

CLEAN THE CUT
Run cut under cool water; this might hurt but the cut needs to be clean.

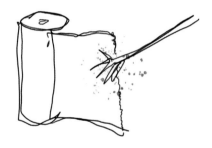

DRY THE CUT
Use clean paper towel to clean and dry the cut, especially if it is still bleeding.

COVER THE CUT
When the entire area is clean and dry, get help to put on a clean Band-Aid to protect the cut.

HOT THINGS BURN YOU,

when cooking, ALWAYS

ALWAYS cook with an adult

ALWAYS use a dry pot holder to hold hot handles. Nothing damp or wet.

ALWAYS know where baking soda or a fire extinguisher are located.

three DEGREES of burns

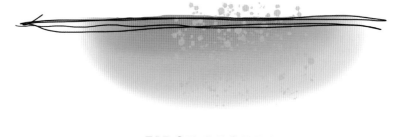

FIRST DEGREE

A little red, a bit swollen. Might hurt for a while.
Your skin might peel a little over the next week as the burn heals.
If it is a large burn, you should go see a doctor.

SECOND DEGREE

Red, swollen, and turning into a blister.
See a doctor if the blister is bigger than 1 inch in diameter.
Immediately run under cold water for at least 15 minutes.
Have a parent or doctor take a look at it.

THIRD DEGREE

Third degree burns don't often happen in a kitchen. Skin
may turn darker brown or white and waxy and form big blisters.
Call 9-1-1 and get immediate medical attention.
The emergency doctor will help you.

3 things to do if you get burned

COLD WATER

Run cold water on the burn immediately and leave it running for 5 minutes.

ASK FOR HELP

You should have someone with you when you are cooking. Ask them to put some ice cubes in a Ziploc bag.

CRY IF YOU WANT TO

If it hurts, go ahead and cry. Sometimes it just feels better.

to STOP a fire

PUT A LID ON IT!

Fires need air to get bigger. Take away the oxygen by putting a lid on top.

SPRINKLE BAKING SODA

Sprinkle lots of baking soda all over the flame to put it out. Don't worry about the mess.

FIRE EXTINGUISHER

If a fire is too big to get close to, use a fire extinguisher.

if there is a fire, DO NOT

DO NOT panic! It is better to stay calm.

DO NOT throw water on it or it will cause an explosion.

DO NOT wave a towel. It may catch on fire and spread the flames.

WHERE are the bad germs?

RAW THINGS

Raw chicken, raw fish, ground meat, unpasteurized dairy

CONTAMINATED FOODS

If raw meat is in contact with other food, it will be contaminated until it is washed or cooked properly.

ON YOUR HANDS

It is crucial to keep your hands clean after you touch things that may have germs.

WHAT happens to you?

UPSET TUMMY

If your tummy is gurgling and you are extra farty, you may have food poisoning.

DIARRHEA OR THROWING UP

If your upset tummy persists, your body may try to get rid of the germs quickly.

FEVER OR HEADACHE

It can make you feel like you are suffering from a flu.

Bacteria, parasites, and viruses

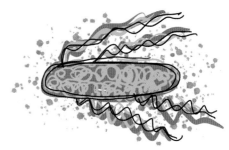

SALMONELLA

Mostly in chicken. It is very important chicken is not pink after being cooked.

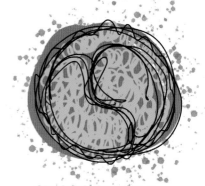

CYCLOSPORA

Found often on imported fruits and vegetables that are not washed before eating

ESCHERICHIA COLI (E.COLI)

Most often associated with raw red meat, it can also be found in fruits and vegetables

AND YOU DON'T WANT THAT!

wash your hands

LOTS OF SUDS

Use warm water and lots of soap to scrub your hands up to the wrist.

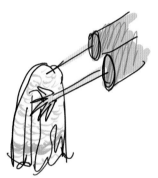

RINSE AND DRY

Rinse the soap off and dry your hands completely.

REPEAT

Any time you touch something that might have germs, wash your hands again.

clean all dirty surfaces

THE SINK

The sink might still be covered in the germs you washed off you hands.

THE HANDLES

Did you touch a knife handle? A drawer handle? The faucet at the sink? You will need to wash those too.

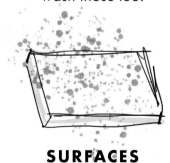

SURFACES

Cutting board, kitchen counter, the refrigerator can all get splattered in germ juice. Keep them clean with disinfectant.

three ways to KILL the germs

HEAT

Meat, chicken, and fish need to be fully cooked to make sure the germs are killed.

CHEMICALS

Use soap on your hands and kitchen disinfectants to clean surfaces.

AVOID CROSS-CONTAMINATION

Is that cloth clean? Is the cutting board germy? Did you touch chicken and then the fridge handle?

THE MUNCHY

MUNCHY BUNCH

focused

always
clean

balanced

serious

always
tasting

organized

follows recipes

mindful

Sal

has to follow the recipe.

She is clean and organized but has trouble if things become out of her control.
She is the best cook in the kitchen as long as everything goes according to plan.

always
joking

too many
ideas

goofy

creative

definitely
messy

silly

enthusiastic

easily
distracted

Pepper

is a hot mess.
He can't follow a recipe without making changes, but things usually work out.
When they don't, it's a huge disaster. He would rather have fun and be creative
than have something turn out perfectly.

Salty

makes everything taste better.

Salt rocks! It's the only rock that we cultivate and eat. Adding salt to something enhances all the good tastes in each ingredient.

feta cheese

ham

bacon

soy sauce

tomato

potato chips

always
hungry

trash
panda

open-
minded

upbeat

ravenous

gassy

Ragu

is always hungry for anything and everything.
He prefers eating more than cooking. When it comes to food, it's all about quantity over quality, and there is no shortage of things to eat in the trash cans.

Bitter

is the least tasty taste.

The way to balance out bitter is to add salt, not sweet. Some cultures think that bitter is better because it is so awful tasting that it must be healthy.

escarole

coffee

bitter melon

grapefruit

tomato

dark chocolate

nope rope

bad vibes

super picky

hangry

grumpy

negative

Ziti

is the absolute most picky eater. Ever. Of all time.
She is best friends with Sal, except no one can figure out why. No one has ever seen her eat anything, which is probably why she is always grumpy.

Sour

makes your mouth pucker.
Sour causes your salivary glands to get drool flowing, in a good way. It's all about finding the sweet and sour balance like in a delicious glass of lemonade.

rhubarb

yogurt

vinegar

lemon

pickle

tomato

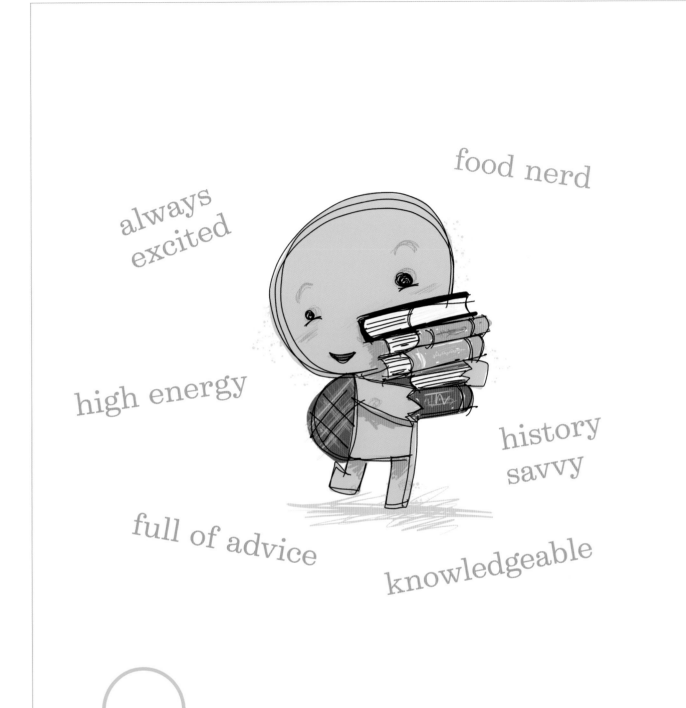

food nerd

always excited

high energy

history savvy

full of advice

knowledgeable

Sage

is the ultimate food nerd.
He knows everything about food history, origin of ingredients, food science, and legends. He has truly fascinating stories to tell even if they are a bit long.

Sweet

is a very attractive taste.
Sugary sweet things have lots of accessible energy for our bodies, so we really crave this taste—even though we know it's not a good idea to have too much sugar.

banana

mango

honey

maple

apple

tomato

busy

brave

always growing

garden master

likes dirt

hard working

Rose

knows how everything grows.

She is constantly busy getting her hands dirty in the garden. Rose is always trying to grow new and wonderful things, and she loves to learn how food gets from the farm to the table.

Umami

is round and delicious.
This big, savory taste makes you feel full and satisfied. When you are craving a piece of cheese or some steak, that's umami.

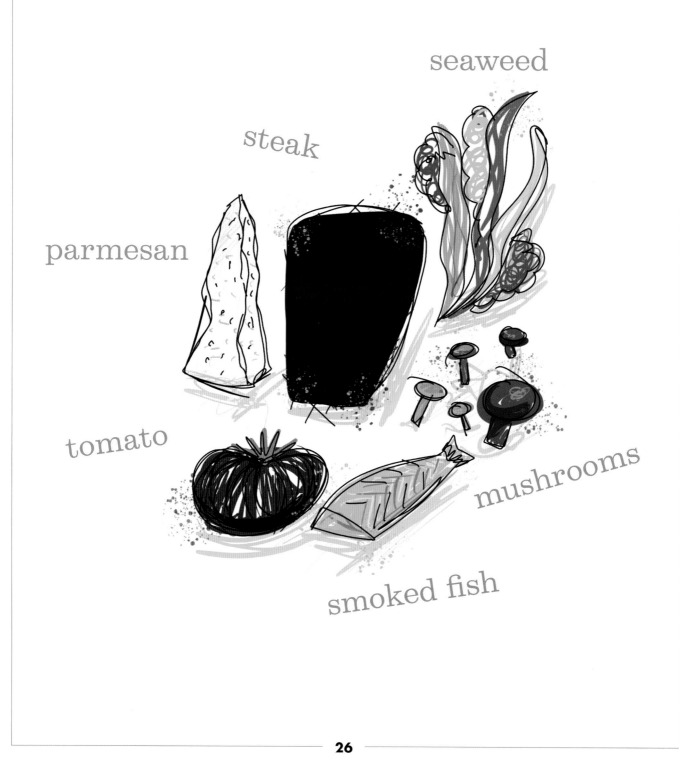

seaweed

steak

parmesan

tomato

mushrooms

smoked fish

global traveler

techie

big on family

multilingual

loves cultures

makes friends easily

Bean

is here and there and everywhere.
She loves to follow online trends to discover her next travel destination so she can experience the culture, language, and food of people from around the world.

ketchup is the best

1 diced onion

sharp

1 Put all ingredients into a medium pot

2 Tbsp sugar

1 clove of garlic

1 can (14 oz) of crushed tomatoes

1 tsp salt

1 Tbsp paprika

1 cup red wine vinegar

hot

2 Cook on low heat with the lid on tight for 1 hour. Stir often to make sure nothing is sticking on the bottom of the pot.

3 Remove the lid. Continue cooking for 30 minutes, stir sometimes, but watch out for splatters!

4 Take the pot off stove and let cool for 30 minutes

how to dice an onion

1 Cut top off onion

2 Shave roots off onion

3 Cut onion in half starting at root end

4 Remove peel

5 Cut ¾ of the way to the root of the onion so it stays connected

6 Cut the other direction until you get to the end and have a pile of diced onion

*Angle each cut slightly to the center of the onion

5 Ladle spoonfuls of the mixture into a blender. Only fill the blender half way.

6 Take the lid off and remove the center cap from the lid

7 Place a DRY cloth over the hole and put the lid back on. Hold the dry cloth while the blender is running.

8 Start the blender on low speed. Slowly increase the speed until it is going full speed. Blend until the mixture is smooth like ketchup…oh wait, it is ketchup.

9 Use a funnel to pour ketchup into a squeeze bottle or any other plastic container

10 Keep in the refrigerator until you need some ketchup

31

BREAKFAST

scrambled eggs

1 Preheat non-stick frying pan over medium-low heat

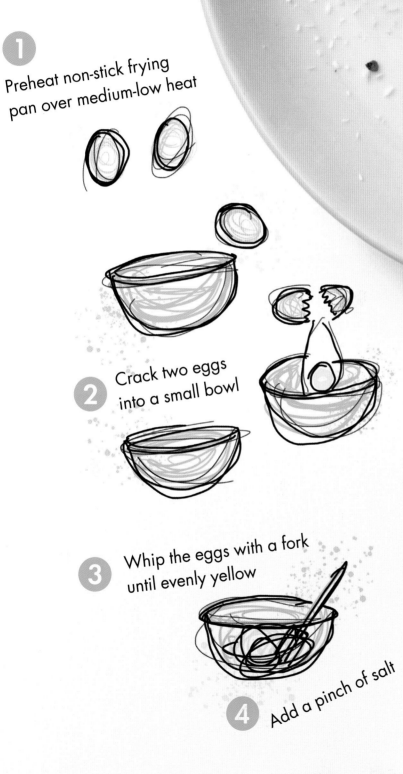

2 Crack two eggs into a small bowl

3 Whip the eggs with a fork until evenly yellow

4 Add a pinch of salt

5 Melt 1 Tbsp butter in the frying pan

6 Pour in the eggs

Use a heat-proof rubber spatula to stir

7 Stir eggs constantly in little circles until they become firm and look like cottage cheese. The more you mix the smaller the little bits of egg will be, so if you only stir a couple times they will be a big piece of egg, but if you stir lots they will be tiny.

8 Remove from heat and add 1 Tbsp of butter, stir until the butter is completely melted

9 Serve eggs warm

Sprinkle eggs with salt and pepper

sunnyside up fried eggs

hot

1 Preheat a non-stick pan on medium-low heat for 5 minutes

2 Crack two eggs into a small bowl, careful not to break the yolk. Remove any egg shells.

3 When pan is hot, add 3 Tbsp cooking oil. Tilt the pan so the oil covers the entire surface.

4 Gently pour the eggs out of the bowl and into the hot oil.

Tilt the bowl away from you in case the oil splashes and keep the bowl close to the pan so the eggs don't fall and crack the yolk.

5 Cook for 5 minutes until the edges of the egg yolk start to turn white instead of transparent

6 Slide the eggs very carefully onto a plate

7 Sprinkle eggs with salt and pepper

boiled eggs
soft or hard

1 Place 2–3 eggs in a small pot with a tight-fitting lid

2 Cover the eggs with cold water so they are totally submerged

3 Bring water to a boil over high heat, when it starts to boil, reduce the heat to medium-low

🔥 hot

4 When the water starts to boil, set the timer for 5 minutes for soft egg yolks or 11 minutes for hard boiled

5 Fill a bowl halfway with ice cubes and water

6 Transfer eggs right into ice water with a slotted spoon

7 Let cool for 10 minutes

8 Crack the egg by tapping it all over against a hard surface

9 Peel the eggs and throw away the shells

10 Cut eggs in half and sprinkle with salt and pepper

41

poached egg

1 Bring a large pot of water to a boil

2 When it boils, add 3 Tbsp of white vinegar (or any kind of vinegar)

3 Crack each egg into a small bowl

4 When the water boils, reduce the heat to medium-low

5 Stir the water around in the pot until a little whirlpool forms

6 Quickly, while the water is still moving, add each egg by tipping it out of the bowl and into the moving water

hot

7 Set a timer for 4 minutes for runny eggs or 6 minutes for firm egg yolks

8 When the timer goes, lift them out of the water with a slotted spoon so the water drips off

9 Sprinkle with salt and pepper

volcano eggs

1
Preheat oven to **450°F** 232°C

2 Get 2 eggs, separate egg white from egg yolk

Working over a small bowl, crack the egg

Pass the yolk gently back and forth between shells

Let the egg whites all fall into the bowl

3 If the egg yolk is unbroken, keep it in the shell

4 If the egg yolk breaks, you have to start separating again with a fresh bowl and egg.

(Just save that broken egg for scrambled eggs.)

5 Beat the egg whites until they form stiff peaks

6 Spoon egg whites into 2 tall piles on a parchment-lined baking sheet. Leave some egg white in the bowl.

7 Make an indent in the egg whites

8 Put one egg yolk into the indent; top with the remaining egg whites so the yolks are completely covered

9 Bake for **10** minutes

hot

10 Let cool for 3 minutes, carefully transfer to a plate to serve

eggs and...

Draw an egg around your top 3 favorite things to eat with your eggs

fresh herbs

ham

sausage

bacon

potatoes

asparagus

pancakes

toast

english muffin

waffle

47

Maple water slowly drips out of a maple tree and collects in a hanging bucket.

Maple water is clear and slightly sweet.

It takes 150L of maple
water to slowly simmer
and thicken into just 1L
of super sweet syrup!

The maple leaf is
a Canadian icon.
So are pancakes!

maple syrup

pancakes

1 In one bowl, combine "wet ingredients"

2 cups milk

2 eggs

2 Tbsp vegetable oil

Whisk together

2 In another bowl, combine "dry ingredients"

2 cups flour   2 Tbsp sugar

2 tsp baking powder

½ tsp salt

Whisk together

3 Pour "wet ingredients" into bowl of "dry ingredients" while whisking until a smooth batter forms

Some lumps are okay

hot

4 Preheat non-stick frying pan on medium heat for 3 minutes

5 When you are ready, add 1 Tbsp butter to the pan. When butter melts, pour ½ cup batter into the pan.

Drop down some tasty flavor nuggets

7 When 6 bubbles pop on the top surface of your pancake,

flip it over using a flat, heat-proof flipper

8 Continue cooking the other side for 1 minute

9 Stack pancakes on a plate, smear on some butter, and pour on lots of maple syrup

fresh blueberries

chocolate chips

banana bits

peanut butter + jam breakfast cookies

Keep a plastic bag full of baked cookies in the freezer for mornings when you accidentally sleep in

52

1 Preheat oven to **350°F** 177°C

🔥 hot

2 In one bowl, mix together "wet ingredients"' until smooth and creamy

½ cup melted butter

¼ cup peanut butter or other nut butter

½ cup brown sugar

½ cup maple syrup

3 Stir in 3 eggs, one at a time, until smooth

4 In another bowl, combine "dry ingredients"

1 cup flour

2 Tbsp flax seeds

2 tsp cinnamon

½ tsp salt

1 tsp baking powder

1 cup chopped walnuts

2 cups instant oats

½ cup cranberries

5 Add "dry ingredients" to "wet ingredients" and mix using a strong spoon

6 Use an ice cream scoop make 16 large piles of sticky cookie batter on 2 parchment-lined baking sheets

7 Make small indent on top of each pile and fill with 1 tsp of your favorite jam

8 Bake for **15** minutes

9 Let cookies cool for 25 minutes

53

nut
butter

1 Preheat oven to **300°F** 150°C

hot

2 Scatter 2 cups of raw nuts on a parchment-lined baking sheet. Try using peanuts, almonds, or cashews, or combine them together.

3 Bake for **25** minutes

4 Put warm toasted nuts into a food processor

1 Tbsp sugar

½ tsp salt

¼ cup vegetable oil

5 Blend for 2 minutes, scrape down the sides with a spatula

6 Blend 2 minutes scrape down sides

7 Blend 5 minutes, scrape down sides

sharp

The food processor blade is not attached to the bowl, so it can fall out when you pour the nut butter out. Remove the very sharp blade before pouring.

8 Pour smooth nut butter into a jar with a lid, refrigerate

berry jam

1. Fill a medium pot

3 cups of frozen berries
1 cup sugar
1 Tbsp lemon juice

2. Put a lid on tight

hot

3. Cook on low heat for 1 hour

4. Remove lid and cook for 1 more hour. Stir every 15 minutes, scrape the bottom of the pot so it does not burn.

5. Remove the pot from heat, let jam cool for 30 minutes in the pot

6. Scoop jam into glass jar and keep it in the fridge it will stay fresh for a month

how to dice an apple

sharp

1

Slice 2 slices off one side of the apple.
Stack the slices on top of each other.

2

Place apple on the flat side.

3

Slice 2 slices off one side. Stack the slices.

4

Slices 2 slices off the other side.
Stack the slices.

5

Tip apple over onto flat side and slice
2 slices off the apple.
Stack the slices and discard the core.

6

Cut slices into strips. Cut strips into cubes.

salsa de frutas

1 Cut 10 strawberries into small pieces and place in a bowl

2 Add 1 diced apple

sharp

3 Add zest and juice of 1 lime

4 Add 10 mint leaves torn into small pieces

5 Mix and set aside

RECIPE CONTINUES...

bananamole

1 Peel and mash 3 bananas with a fork in a bowl

2 Add

1 Tbsp cocoa powder

2 Tbsp brown sugar

1 Tbsp olive oil

½ tsp ground cinnamon

pinch of salt

3 Mix with fork until mixture is evenly brown. Lumps are okay

dulce fundido

1 In a bowl combine

½ can of dulce de leche

1 cup of plain yogurt

2 Whisk until smooth

breakfast nachos

Scatter a bag of corn tortillas on a large platter

Top with scattered scoops of bananamole, dulce fundido, and salsa de frutas

dulce fundido

bananamole

salsa de frutas

59

LUNCH

cheesy puns...

63

very,
very, very slow
grilled cheese

1 Preheat a non-stick pan on the lowest heat on the stove. Low temperature is very important.

2 Spread soft butter on two pieces of bread.

If your butter is cold, microwave it for 20 seconds to soften.

3 Start stacking

First piece of bread, butter side down

A processed cheese slice for extra meltiness

Grate a bit of your favorite cheddar cheese

Tear up soft little bocconcini balls

Another processed cheese slice on top

The other piece of buttered bread with butter side facing up

5 Place sandwich carefully in non-stick frying pan on the lowest heat.

It's okay if some of the cheese bits fall out of the sandwich.

6 Cook for 10 minutes:

set a timer and walk away from the pan

8 Let the sandwich cool for 5 minutes so the cheese becomes the perfect melty

hot

7 Carefully flip the sandwich and cook for another 10 minutes on the other side

9 Use a serrated knife to cut so the cheese doesn't squish out

sharp

bakin' bacon perfection

1 Preheat oven to **350°F** 177°C

2 Place a piece of parchment paper on a baking sheet

3 Arrange 1 package of bacon slices on parchment paper without overlapping the slices

4 Bake for **35** minutes

5 Move slices of bacon using tongs to a plate lined with a few pieces of paper towel; the bacon will get crispier as it cools

WARNING:
Hold on! watch out for hot liquid like bacon fat. If your oven mitt gets wet from bacon fat, it can burn right through the glove to your hand instantly.

hot

bacon, lettuce, and tomato

Let go of my bacon!

It's the bacon or your arm!

RECIPE CONTINUES...

1 Pick a head of lettuce that is clean and green

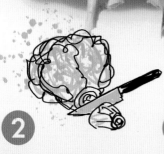

2 Cut the bottom off the head of lettuce and pull the leaves apart

3 Wash the leaves under cold running water to rinse of any garden grit

4 Pile leaves into a salad spinner and spin to remove extra water

1 Choose a juicy, bright red tomato

sharp

2 Don't press down when you slice a tomato or it will squish the juice out and wreck the tomato

3 Slide your knife forwards and backwards like a saw to cut through the tomato

4 Make all the slices the same thickness

build a BLT

hot

1 Put two slices of bread in the toaster to turn them into toast

2 Smear mayonnaise on each piece of toast

3 Stack 2 big pieces of lettuce and 4 pieces of bacon on one side

4 Layer enough juicy tomato slices on the other side

5 Top with lots of salt and black pepper

6 Squash the sandwich together

whisk-y moves

zigzag
Move the whisk in a crisscross back and forth across the bowl

eighty-eight
Trace a figure 8 shape over and over itself

around in circles
Whirl the whisk in circles around the edge of the bowl and into the mixture

caesar salad dressing

1 One fresh egg at room temperature

2 Crack the egg on the side of a small bowl

3 Carefully pass egg yolk back and forth while egg white falls into a small bowl

4 Put the egg yolk into a large bowl

5 Add 1 tsp Dijon mustard

6 Whisk with one hand

7 Add oil a spoonful at a time with the other hand

½ cup vegetable oil mixed with ½ cup olive oil

8 Whisk smooth before adding each new spoonful of oil it will get thicker and thicker

Keep the bowl from wobbling by setting it into a snug-fitting pot

9 Turn the mayonnaise into salad dressing

zest of 1 lemon

Zest is the yellow part of the lemon skin, don't grate the white part

juice 1 lemon

1 clove of garlic, peeled and grated on a zester

2 splashes of Worcestershire sauce

3 Tbsp grated parmesan cheese

fresh cracked pepper

RECIPE CONTINUES...

crunchy croutons

1 Preheat oven to **300°F** 150°C

2 Cut 2 pieces of frozen white bread into strips

Use a serrated knife and frozen bread so you don't tear the bread

sharp

3 Cut the strips into squares

4 Toss bread cubes in a bowl with 2 Tbsp olive oil and ¼ tsp salt

5 Spread bread cubes on a parchment-lined baking sheet

6 Bake for **20** minutes

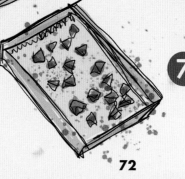

7 Remove from oven and let croutons cool for 20 minutes

caesar salad

1 Remove all the leaves from 1 head of romaine lettuce and discard the center part when the leaves get too small

2 Use your hands to tear the leaves into bite-sized pieces, throw away the bits of brown lettuce

3 Put lettuce in a large bowl only add half the dressing

4 Toss the salad until the leaves are evenly covered

5 Taste a piece of lettuce and decide if you think it should have more dressing

6 Serve in bowls topped with parmesan cheese, crunchy croutons, and fresh cracked pepper

sharp

underground round up of roots and tubers

beet

Sweet beets are big and juicy. They are mostly found red or golden. Red beets will stain hands red.

potato

Everybody loves potatoes. They come in all shapes and sizes and colors. But no matter how you slice them, they are all some tasty taters.

parsnip

Look just like a big carrot, but taste even sweeter than a carrot when roasted

sweet potato

Sweet potatoes come in different colors from white to orange to purple. They all taste a little different, but they are all soft and sticky and sweet when roasted. They can be very huge!

carrot

Carrots come in all kinds of different colors other than orange. They can be purple, yellow, red, or even white.

roast roots

1 Preheat oven to **375°F** 190°C

2 Choose any assortment of roots from parsnips, potatoes, beets, carrots, sweet potatoes.

sharp

3 Peel all root vegetables

4 Cut the root vegetables into bite-sized pieces

5 Scatter the mixed roots onto a parchment paper–lined baking sheet all in one even layer

hot

6 Bake for **45** minutes

until caramelized and soft when pressed with a fork

9 Pour all the roasted roots into a large bowl

7 While they roast, make a simple sweet vinaigrette (next page)

10 Add some of the vinaigrette. Mix it all around and taste. Add more vinaigrette needed.

8 Let roots cool for 15 minutes

11 Serve the roots warm, or room temperature, or chilled in the fridge

RECIPE CONTINUES...

a super simple vinaigrette

1 Place all ingredients into a glass jar with a lid

¼ cup of balsamic vinaigrette

3 Tbsp maple syrup

1 Tbsp of mustard
(any kind you have will work)

¾ cup vegetable oil

½ tsp salt

fresh pepper

2 Secure lid and shake the jar until the vinaigrette is smooth

3 Taste it now and add more salt or vinegar to adjust the seasoning

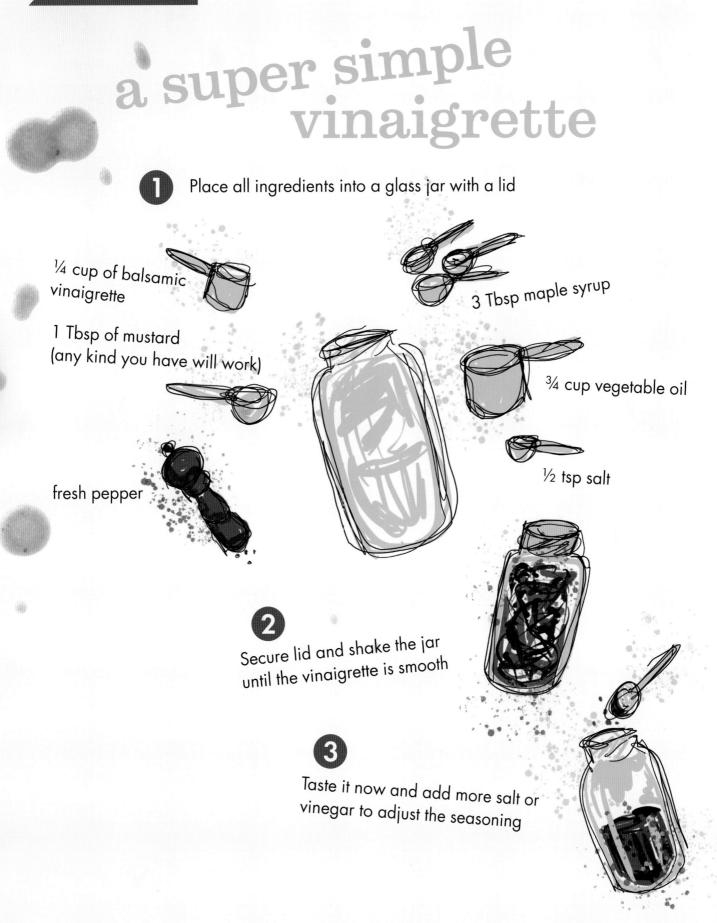

pumpkin patch pals

INSIDE COLOR RANGE

acorn

Lots of cool looking ridges and chewy edible skin make this a fun squash to eat roasted plain.

butternut

Butternut squash has the most amount of "meat" inside. Probably the most popular squash to eat.

hubbard

Big, nubbly, and covered in bumps. The green ones are called blue and the orange ones are called golden.

Pumpkins (and other winter squash) are savory and sweet, which makes them really great to eat for dinner or dessert. It's a perfect balance of tastes.

A winter squash has a tough outer skin and will keep growing even when the weather begins to cool down. Summer squash are thin skinned and don't like the cold.

There are hundreds of different winter squash with pretty fun names.

kabocha

Dark orange insides taste really yummy and toasty. Roast kabocha gets a bit dry and crumbly but tastes really good.

spaghetti

Roast spaghetti squash goes all soft and stringy and looks like spaghetti.

pumpkin

Small, big, giant. Orange, white, green. Pumpkins come in all shapes and sizes.

Winter squash are very heavy and wobbly and dangerous to cut with a knife...so here is a fun and safe way to break down your squash!

how to squash a squash

1 Place a squash on a tea towel

2 Collect the four corners of the tea towel together and hold them tightly

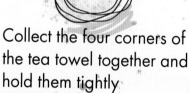

3 Smash the pumpkin hard on the ground

4 Smash until it breaks into large chunks

how to roast a squash

1 Choose a squash

2 Preheat oven to **375°F** 190°C

3 Squash the squash

4 Place chunks on a parchment-lined baking sheet

hot

5 Scrape the pumpkin guts and seeds off into a bowl

6 Bake for **60** minutes

7 Remove from oven and let cool for 30 minutes

8 Scoop the soft pumpkin skin away from the hard outer skin and discard the tough skin

9 Eat the squash with plain butter and salt or turn it into a pumpkin pie soup

RECIPE CONTINUES...

toasted pumpkin seeds

1 Preheat oven to **375°F** 190°C

2 Remove all the gunk from the seeds and place them in a sieve or colander

3 Rinse them really well and shake out all the liquid

5 Grab handfuls and scatter onto a parchment-lined baking sheet in one even layer

4 Put seeds into a bowl
1 Tbsp sugar
big pinch of salt
2 Tbsp olive oil
Mix to coat evenly

6 Shake pan slightly so seeds lay flat and don't overlap

hot

7 Bake for **30** minutes

8 Let them cool for 30 minutes

whipped cream

1 In a large bowl whisk 1 cup of whipping cream

2 Keep whisking until the cream becomes very thick; it is ready when it holds on to the whisk

pumpkin pie soup

1 Place soft roasted squash into a blender

2 Add water so it covers the pile of squash pieces

3 Add pumpkin spices:

2 tsp cinnamon

¼ tsp ground cloves

1 tsp ground ginger

½ tsp ground cardamom

pinch of allspice

pinch of ground nutmeg

1 Tbsp of apple cider vinegar

big pinch of salt

4 Take the lid off and remove the center cap from the lid

Place a DRY cloth over the hole and put the lid back on

5 Put a lid on blender. Blend until smooth. If the soup is too thick, add more water.

hot

6 Pour in a pot and heat slowly over medium heat until it simmers

7 Serve with a dollop of whipped cream and some crunchy toasted pumpkin seeds

85

DINNER

iceberg lettuce

1 Hold a head of iceberg lettuce in both hands with the stem facing downwards

2 Smash the bottom stem of the lettuce hard onto a clean counter

3 Now remove the loose stem easily in one big piece

4 Pry the head of lettuce open and separate into big leaves

5 Stack two leaves together into a cup shape and arrange the cups on large platter or serving tray

soy delicious lettuce wraps

2 Cut a brick of firm tofu into small cubes
it is easy to cut

1 Place a large non-stick frying pan over medium heat

hot

3 Add 1 Tbsp vegetable oil to the pan

4 Gently place all the tofu pieces into the hot oil
do not move the tofu, just let it fry for 7 minutes

5 Add the following and cook for 5 minutes:

3 green onions, finely sliced

3 big slices of ginger

2 cloves of garlic

sharp

1 carrot, peeled and grated

6 Then add the following:

¼ cup soy sauce

2 Tbsp brown sugar

¼ cup of water

1 cup of frozen edamame beans

2 Tbsp vinegar

7 Cook until most of the liquid has evaporated, about 7 minutes

8 Remove from heat to cool for 10 minutes

9 When the tofu mixture has cooled down, remove the garlic and ginger chunks

RECIPE CONTINUES...

lettuce choose our own adventure

Serve everything in little bowls
so everyone can build their own

sriracha hot sauce

sweet hoisin sauce

fresh picked basil leaves

bowl of tofu mixture

a pile of lettuce leaves

slices of lime

sesame seeds

made with soy

edamame
Soy beans grow in pods, they are often served steamed or boiled with salt or soy sauce as a snack

meat alternatives
Tofu, tempeh, textured vegetable protein, vegetarian hotdogs, vegetarian "chicken" nuggets, and many more

miso
A fermented paste used to add big umami flavor to foods

soy milk
A dairy-free milk substitute for people who cannot digest dairy

soy sauce
There are many kinds of sauce that feature soy: light soy, dark soy, sweet soy, hoisin, tamari, shoyu, teriyaki

92

SCHNITZEL LEVEL 1	SCHNITZEL LEVEL 2	SCHNITZEL LEVEL 3
First you must carefully hammer them flat...	Then you must bread them all over...	Finally you must fry them properly in hot oil...
...without contaminating the entire kitchen with raw meat germs!	...without making a huge mess and contaminating the kitchen again.	...without starting a fire or burning yourself and the schnitzel!

Only the best chefs are worthy to wield the hammer of schnitzel!

95

flatten pork chops

 1 Place a pork chop in the center of a large, heavy-duty resealable plastic bag. Do not seal the bag.

 2 Slowly tap the pork chop with a meat hammer.

This can take a while. Don't hit it super hard. If you whack too hard, it can tear a hole in the meat or even in the plastic bag. Tap evenly over the entire surface. Do 20–25 whacks.

Meat hammers can be all metal or have a wooden handle. The hammer usually has a flat side and a bumpy side. Just use the flat side, the bumpy side will tear the plastic bag.

 3 Flip over and continue to pound evenly all over. Do another 20–25 whacks.

 4 Flip over one more time and hammer until the meat is evenly thin all over

5 Place the flattened pork chops on a plate to get ready for breading

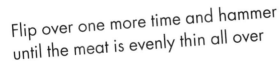

 6 Repeat the process 5 times for a total of 6 pork chops

RECIPE CONTINUES...

breading pork chops

Set up a breading station with three shallow dishes:

DISH #1

1 cup all-purpose flour

1 tsp salt

DISH #2

4 eggs, beaten

2 Tbsp milk

DISH #3

2 cups panko bread crumbs

To make sure both your hands don't end up getting really messy and causing the chops to get super gross, assign each hand to be either wet or dry

1 Wet hand picks up the pork chop and places it into the flour

DISH #1

2 Dry hand sprinkles flour all over the pork chop, covering it completely

3 Dry hand picks up the floury pork chop and gently lays it into the egg mixture

4 Wet hand picks up the eggy chop and flips it over to make sure it is completely covered in egg mixture

DISH #2

5 Wet hand holds up the pork chop to let any extra egg drip off

6 Wet hand gently places the pork chop onto the bread crumbs

7 Dry hand sprinkles bread crumbs on the pork chop

8 Dry hand flips the chop over and presses the bread crumbs into the chop so it is completely covered

germs

DISH #3

9 Dry hand picks up breaded pork chop and puts it onto the tray or cutting board to wait for frying

RECIPE CONTINUES...

frying schnitzel

hot

Choose either a heavy cast-iron frying pan or a non-stick frying pan

1 Fill a large frying pan with ¼ inch of frying oil

2 Warm oil over medium-low heat for 5 minutes

3 Place a breaded pork chop schnitzel into the oil using a pair of tongs to hold it. Be careful about splashing hot oil onto yourself.

You can fill the pan with schnitzels, but do not overlap the schnitzels.

4 Fry on each side for about 10 minutes or until the bread crumbs become golden brown and crispy. Flip using tongs.

5 Remove crispy schnitzel from the pan and place on a piece of paper towel on a plate

6 Add more oil to the pan and keep frying until they are all done

7 Serve with a slice of lemon to squeeze on top

hard herbs

Hard herbs usually need a bit of cooking to activate their aroma. They can also be a bit tougher, so cooking helps to soften them and make them easier and more pleasant to eat.

You definitely don't want to eat the stems, they are too tough.

sage

rosemary

thyme

oregano

soft herbs

Soft herbs can be munched up raw, used as a garnish on top of food, or mixed into something hot at the last minute.

They are more delicate and should be left whole or slightly hand torn into smaller pieces.

Remove the delicate leaves from the stems and get rid of the tough stem part.

chives

cilantro

dill

parsley

mint

basil

These are only a few kinds of herbs. There are many, many more to discover.

herby chicken stew

1 Peel and cut vegetables into large chunks

Peel and cut 2 carrots

sharp

Peel and cut 2 red potatoes

Peel and cut 1 onion

Cut 2 celery stalks

2 Melt ¼ cup butter in a large pot on medium-low heat

hot

3 Add vegetables.
Cook for 10 minutes.

4 Chop 2 Tbsp of any kind of hard herbs into very fine specks

Remove the leaves, throw away the stems

Cut the leaves until they are very fine using a slow and steady rocking motion on the cutting board

sharp

RECIPE CONTINUES...

5 Cut 6 boneless, skinless chicken thighs into large pieces

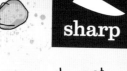

6 Place the chicken chunks into the pot. Stir it all up and cook for 5 more minutes.

7 Add 4 cups milk and reduce heat to low. Stir so everything is evenly distributed.

8 Cook on low with no lid for 1 hour. Stir every 10 minutes to make sure nothing is burning or sticking on the bottom of the pot.

9

Stir in 1 cup heavy cream
and 1 cup hand-torn soft herbs
at the very last moment.
Add more salt, if needed.

10

Serve immediately. If you
feel like adding even more
herbs, tear up some soft
herbs as a garnish on top.

masala dabba

"Masala dabba" means "spice box."
They are usually round metal tins with a glass top.
Inside are seven little metal cups filled with spices or
spice blends used to make curries like butter chicken.

Put any whole-seed or
ground-powder spices
in a masala dabba
or

use pre-mixed
spice blends

coriander cumin powder
red chili cumin seeds
cardamom mustard seed
fenugreek turmeric

garam masala

is a spice blend
made of other spices.
The word "garam"
means "warm"
the word "masala"
means "spice blend."

Garam masala
can come in lots of
flavors depending
on what spices are
used to make it.

practice guessing
which spice is which
with closed eyes by
only smelling

These are only a few kinds
of spices. There are many,
many more to discover.

109

butter chicken

1 Cut 4 large boneless, skinless chicken breasts into large chunks

2 Place the chicken chunks in a large resealable plastic bag

3 Add the following to the bag:

2 cloves of garlic, grated

zest of 1 lemon and the juice

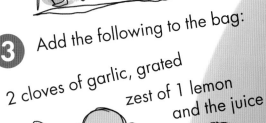

1 cup plain Greek yogurt

4 Seal the bag. Mush up the chicken to make sure everything is evenly mixed.

5 Marinate in the refrigerator for 2 hours or overnight

5 Preheat oven to **375°F** 191°C

6 Arrange chicken chunks on a parchment paper–lined baking sheet in a single layer

7 Bake for **10** minutes

8 Remove chicken from the oven

hot

9 Preheat oven to **BROIL**

Broil means the heat in the oven is extra hot and comes from the top down

10 Place baking sheet on the top rack in the oven

11 Broil for 5 minutes to make black-charred specks

12 Remove from the oven and let it cool while you make the sauce

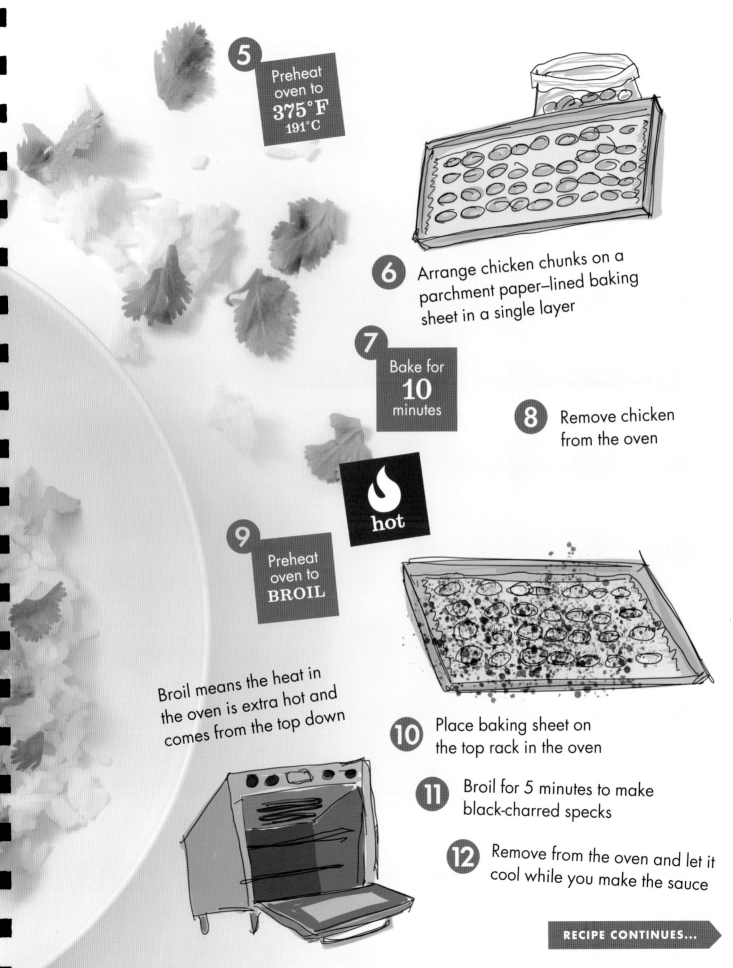

RECIPE CONTINUES...

hot

1 Melt ½ cup butter in a large pot on low heat

1 tsp ground turmeric

1 Tbsp ground cumin

1 Tbsp ground coriander

1 Tbsp garam masala

⅛ tsp ground red hot chili

2 Cook on low for 10 minutes

3 Carefully add the cooked chicken into the sauce

Add 1 can (14 ounces) crushed tomatoes. Watch out for splashes and splats.

Add 2 cups heavy cream.

4 Cook on low heat for 30 minutes

5

Serve on rice with big
pieces of cilantro plucked
and scattered all over the top

RECIPE FOR PERFECT RICE ▶ GO TO NEXT PAGE

how to make perfect basmati rice

hot

1 Put the kettle on to boil water

2 You will need a pot with a tight-fitting lid

3 Add 1 cup of rice per 2 people

4 Add 2 cups of boiling water for each cup of rice

5 Put the lid on the pot, and cook on low heat. (Don't touch that lid! Don't even peek.) Set a timer for 20 minutes.

6 Turn the heat off, but don't touch the lid! No peeking! Set a timer for 10 minutes.

7 Finally remove the lid. Fluff up rice with a fork and serve warm.

During the ancient Ottoman Empire, they had awesome parties.
The Sultan would invite the best chefs from across the empire
to work together and share ideas, ingredients, and cooking
techniques to create the most elaborate and delicious feasts.
How did they choose the best chefs? A cook-off? A food fight?
Nope. They just had to show they could cook perfect rice.
Everyone always had a rice time!

116

make pizza dough

with a mixer

by hand

1

2 Tbsp active dry yeast

2 cups warm water

2 Tbsp sugar

3 Tbsp olive oil

Leave the ingredients to proof for 10 minutes

1

2 Mix in a stand mixer with the dough hook attachment on low speed

2 Mix with a strong wooden spoon

3 **3** Add 5 cups flour 1 Tbsp salt

4 Let the machine knead the dough on medium speed for 10 minutes

4 When the mixture starts to clump together, scrape everything out of the bowl and onto a clean counter

5 Cover with plastic wrap and let it inflate for 1 hour

CONTINUE TO SHAPING

5 Bring all the scraps of dough together into one ball

6 Lock your arm out straight and put that palm into the dough ball

7 Lean forward keeping your arm straight until the dough ball rolls out to a tube shape

Use extra flour to stop the dough from sticking to your hands

8 Fold the long dough in half. Repeat pressing and folding with your straight arm until the dough ball is super smooth.

9 The dough needs to be kneaded to stretch and become smooth

10 This can take at least ten minutes. It helps to have a friend around to take turns kneading.

The best stretch happens here when you fold the dough over

11 Put the smooth dough ball into a bowl, cover with plastic wrap. Let it inflate for 1 hour.

CONTINUE TO SHAPING

shaping

1 After the dough has inflated, turn the contents of the bowl out onto the counter

2 Use a pastry cutter to divide the dough into 12 equal pieces

3 With cupped hands roll dough in a circle into a smooth, round ball

4 Put on a baking sheet with lots of room between. Rub dough balls with olive oil.

5 Cover tightly with plastic wrap and put in the fridge for at least 2 hours and up to 48 hours

6 Place a dough ball on a piece of parchment paper. Drizzle with olive oil so it doesn't stick to your fingers.

7 Use your fingertips to press the dough to make it flat. Stretch it out into a circle, but don't tear a hole.

8 Place the parchment paper on a baking sheet before topping or it will be impossible to lift

make and bake your custom pizza

1 Preheat oven to **425°F** 218°C

Top with your favorite sauce, cheese, and toppings. The cheese gets extra crispy around the edges, so it's okay to spill the toppings over the edges.

2 sauces

tomato sauce
pesto
alfredo sauce
sour cream
barbecue sauce
tomato salsa

3 toppings

pitted olives
diced tomatoes
sliced zucchini
diced pineapple
diced red peppers

chopped spinach
sliced pepperoni
diced ham
cooked ground beef
arugula
basil leaves

4 cheese

grated gruyère
grated monterey jack
grated parmesan
fresh ricotta
slices of provolone
crumbled feta
grated mozzarella
bocconcini
grated cheddar

5 Bake for **20** minutes

6 Cut into 4 slices using a rolling pizza cutter

sharp

hot

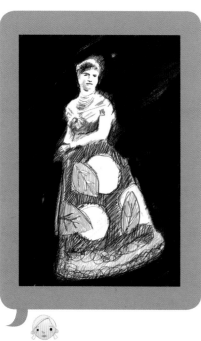

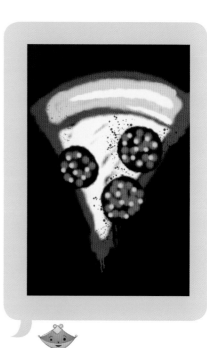

Pietza
Mondrian

Sal's classic Margherita

Named after Queen Margherita, this pizza is topped with ingredients that represent the colors of the Italian flag. Green basil, white bocconcini cheese, and red tomato sauce.

fresh basil leaves

bocconcini

tomato sauce

Garnish with fresh basil leaves

grated mozzarella cheese

mini pepperoni sticks, sliced

regular pepperoni slices

big pepperoni slices

tomato sauce

Pepper packed a pepperoni pizza

Pepperoni is the greatest pizza topping of all time. But pepperoni comes in all shapes and sizes, so how do you decide which kind to use? Use them all. All the pepperonis!

Rose goes green

grated parmesan cheese

dollops of pesto ricotta

zucchini slices

Combine

1 cup ricotta and 2 scoops of pesto

To make pesto

4 cups fresh basil leaves

1 cup olive oil

½ cup water

2 cloves of garlic

½ cup pinenuts

Blend all ingredients until smooth

Garnish with fresh arugula

Ragu's busting at the seams calzone

A calzone is a folded pizza filled with pizza deliciousness.

cooked Italian sausage
sauteed onions
sauteed sweet peppers
tomato sauce of choice
mini bocconcini cheese balls

Only put filling on half the dough, and leave a clean edge all the way around to seal in the yummy ingredients.

Fold the pizza in half; pinch the edge together

Roll the seam over, pinching more as you go

TAKES LONGER TO BAKE THAN PIZZA

Bake for **40** minutes

Drizzle with olive oil salt and dried herbs

Garnish with

green onions, sliced

sour cream

grated cheddar cheese

corn kernels

black beans

tomato salsa

Bean's burrito pizza

It's extra tasty to combine different food from around the world.
It's a pizza, it's a burrito, it's both, and it's double delicious.

Sage's flammkuchen

Sage was inspired by wood-fire baked pizza from Alsace, France.

fresh thyme leaves

grated gruyère cheese

plain potato chips

prosciutto

thin slices of
granny smith apple

sour cream

Scoville scale

The Scoville scale tells you how hot your chili pepper is based on how much capsaicin it contains. Capsaicin is a chemical that makes your mouth feel like it's on fire. It can also hurt your eyes and skin if you come into contact with it.

Scotch bonnet	100,000–300,000
red & green Thai	50,000–100,000
serrano	10,000–23,000
jalapeño	2,500–8,000
sweet bell	0

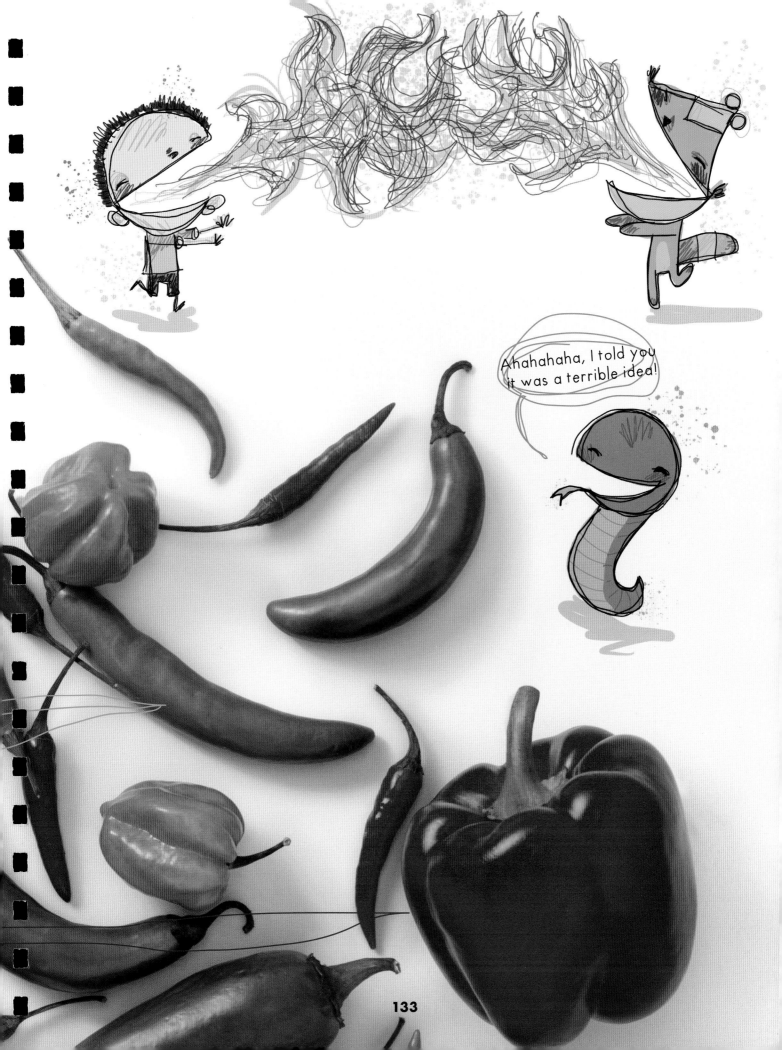

133

veggie prep to make veggie chili

Cut 3 green onions into small pieces

Throw away the roots

Put green pieces in a bowl to garnish later

Light green parts get cooked in the chili

Peel 1 carrot

Cut carrot into short rounds, throw away the ends

Split rounds in half and split them in half again

Cut sticks into dice

Trim the ends off a stalk of celery

Cut the celery in half

Cut into long strips

Cut strips into dice

2 sweet bell peppers

Cut peppers in half and pull out the seeds. Throw away the seeds and stem.

Cut peppers into strips

Dice them up

CONTINUE TO SHAPING

...RECIPE CONTINUED

veggie chili

1 Get a large pot over medium heat

2 Tbsp butter

Add diced celery, carrot, green onion, and bell pepper

*cutting instructions on page 135

2 Sautee for 20 minutes, stirring occasionally

hot

sharp

3 Use the Scoville scale to decide which chili pepper to use.

Split the chili in half to make it easier to remove any time it starts to make the chili too spicy.

4 Add tomatoes, beans, and chili powder

2 Tbsp chili powder

1 can (14 oz) of mixed beans (liquid and beans)

5 Cook over medium heat for 30 minutes

1 can (14 oz) of crushed tomatoes

7 Serve with

grated cheese

green onions

sour cream

6 Remove the spicy chili pepper so no one gets a spicy surprise

MINI CORNBREAD MUFFINS ▷ GO TO NEXT PAGE

simple mini cornbread muffins

1 Preheat oven to **375°F** 190°C

2 Combine "wet ingredients" in one bowl

1 egg

¼ cup melted butter

¾ cup milk

1 Tbsp white vinegar

3 Combine "dry ingredients" in another bowl

½ cup cornmeal

½ cup flour

1 tsp baking soda

¼ tsp salt

4 Add "dry ingredients" to "wet ingredients" and whisk until smooth

hot

5 Spray a muffin tin with non-stick spray so the muffins don't stick

6 Use a mini ice cream scoop to fill the muffin tin

7 Bake for **20** minutes

8 Let muffins cool for 10 minutes before carefully popping them out with a fork

139

SWEETS

chocolate brownie

1 Preheat oven to **350°F** 177°C

2 Combine the following dry ingredients in a large bowl:

½ cup flour

⅓ cup cocoa powder

1½ tsp baking powder

¼ tsp salt

3 Whisk the wet ingredients together in another bowl until very smooth:

½ cup melted butter

1 cup white sugar

2 eggs

4 Combine wet and dry mixtures

5 Cut parchment paper to fit into an 8 × 8-inch baking pan with overhanging flaps

6 Brush the pan well with melted butter

7 Spread the thick batter evenly in the pan

hot

8 Bake for **35** minutes

9 Let the brownie cool down in the pan for 10 minutes

10 Use a dinner knife to make sure the edges are not stuck to the pan. Lift brownie out of the pan using the parchment paper flaps.

RECIPE CONTINUES...

macerated strawberries

sharp

1. Pick 20 firm, bright red, juicy strawberries

2. Trim off the green tops and cut strawberries in half

3. Put all the cut strawberries into a large resealable plastic bag. Add 2 Tbsp brown sugar.

4. Seal bag and mash the strawberries gently with your hands until the sugar melts

vanilla whipped cream

1 Pour 1 cup cold heavy cream (35% milk fat) into a large bowl.

2 Whisk . . . a lot. Whisk until the cream becomes thick enough to stand up on its own.

3 Add the seeds from half a vanilla bean, ½ cup sour cream, and 1 cup icing sugar.

sharp

4 Whisk until the little black vanilla flecks are evenly distributed throughout the white cream.

How to remove the sticky black vanilla bean seeds:

With a small knife, slowly split the vanilla pod down the middle.

Use the side of the knife to scrape out the sticky, tiny black seeds.

Save the scraped bean pods in a jar of white sugar to make vanilla sugar.

butter

Room temperature to cream properly with the sugar. Works with sugar and egg to create the chewy texture.

1 STICK IS EQUAL TO ½ CUP

chocolate chip cookies

Follow the steps to make perfect chocolate chip cookies. Learn what each ingredient does to the final cookie texture. Experiment with changing the amount of some ingredients to get different results.

1 Preheat oven to **350°F** 177°C

sugar

Brown, white, or a combination of both. Adding more sugar makes the cookie chewier.

RANGE ½ CUP TO 1 CUP

2 Cream together room-temperature butter and sugar in bowl.

Creaming means mixing sugar and butter until smooth and lighter in color.

eggs

Room temperature. Egg is the soft sticky glue that holds it all together.

1 OR 2 EGGS

3 Add egg(s) and mix evenly.

extract

Vanilla is traditional but experiment with flavors like: maple, almond, or banana.

4 Add extract. Mix in.

1 TEASPOON OF EXTRACT

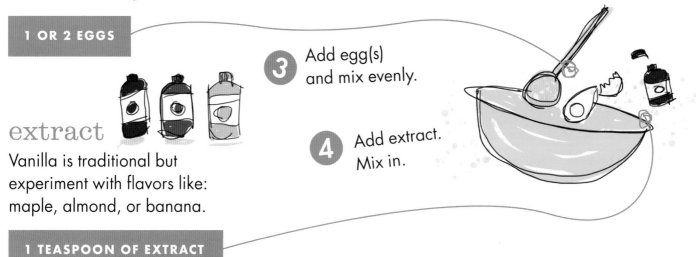

5 In the another bowl, combine flour, baking soda, and salt.

6 Add the dry ingredients into the wet ingredients. Mix very carefully with a wooden spoon.

The dough is tough to mix, but it needs to be mixed evenly.

7 Mix in the chocolate chips.

8 Use a small ice cream scoop or spoon to scoop out evenly sized balls of cookie dough.

9 Place dough balls on a parchment paper–lined baking sheet with enough space between each ball so they can expand without getting stuck together

10 Bake for **10** minutes

hot

11 Let cookies cool for 20 minutes before eating

flour
All-purpose, whole wheat, or a combination of both. Flour gives the cookie structure and makes it more solid.

¾ CUP TO 1¼ CUPS

baking soda
Causes a chemical reaction to help the cookie puff up and rise.

¼ TO 1 TEASPOOON

salt
Any kind of a fine-grain salt. Makes all the flavors taste better.

1 PINCH

chocolate chips
Milk chocolate, semi-sweet, or chocolate chunks. Without chocolate chips, it's just a cookie.

1 CUP

3 variations of
chocolate chip cookies

	classic	cakey	chewy
butter	1 stick	1 stick	1 stick
sugar	¼ cup sugar ¼ cup brown sugar	¼ cup sugar ¼ cup brown sugar	¼ cup sugar ¾ cup brown sugar
egg(s)	1 egg	2 eggs	1 egg
vanilla extract	1 teaspoon	1 teaspoon	1 teaspoon
flour	1 cup flour	1 ¼ cups flour	¾ cup flour
baking soda	¼ teaspoon	1 teaspoon	¼ teaspoon
salt	1 pinch	1 pinch	1 pinch
chocolate chips	1 cup	1 cup	1 cup
raw dough		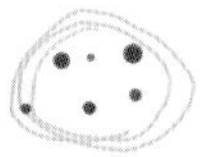	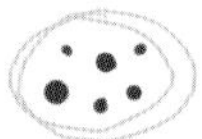
baked cookie	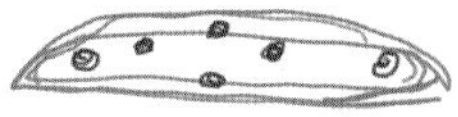	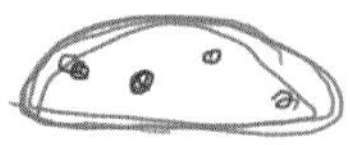	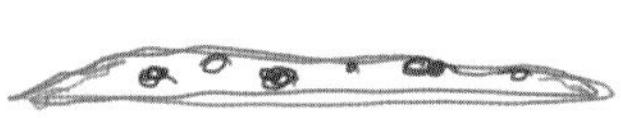

I prefer my chocolate chip cookies warm from the oven with a glass of cold milk.

I like my chocolate chip cookies frozen with a cup of hot cocoa.

I don't like
chocolate chip
cookies.

I enjoy chocolate chip
cookies on a fancy plate.

I want chocolate chip
cookies in my face!

I like sharing
chocolate chip cookies
with new friends.

I love the smell
of freshly baked
chocolate chip cookies.

152

153

peppermint sugar cookies

1 In a bowl, whisk wet ingredients:

1 cup butter, half melted

1½ cups sugar

1 egg

1 tsp peppermint extract

2 In a separate bowl, combine dry ingredients

2¾ cups all-purpose flour

1 tsp baking soda

½ tsp baking powder

3 Combine the dry ingredients with the wet ingredients

4 The dough is really stiff, so mix it slowly until it all comes together into smooth dough balls without any dry bits

5 Put the dough into a large resealable plastic bag

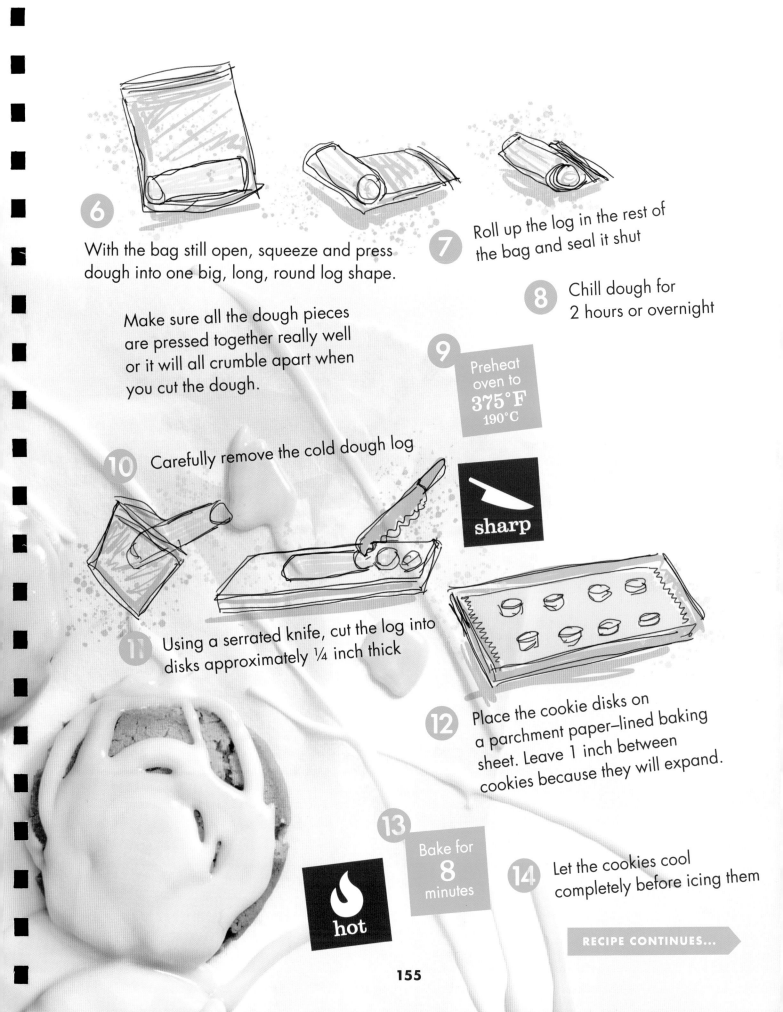

6 With the bag still open, squeeze and press dough into one big, long, round log shape.

Make sure all the dough pieces are pressed together really well or it will all crumble apart when you cut the dough.

7 Roll up the log in the rest of the bag and seal it shut

8 Chill dough for 2 hours or overnight

9 Preheat oven to **375°F** 190°C

10 Carefully remove the cold dough log

sharp

11 Using a serrated knife, cut the log into disks approximately ¼ inch thick

12 Place the cookie disks on a parchment paper–lined baking sheet. Leave 1 inch between cookies because they will expand.

13 Bake for **8** minutes

hot

14 Let the cookies cool completely before icing them

RECIPE CONTINUES...

runny icing for drizzling

1 In a small bowl, combine:

1 cup icing sugar

tablespoon milk

3 drops peppermint extract

2 Stir slowly with a spoon until completely mixed together. The mixture should be a little runny.

If the icing is too runny, add icing sugar.
If it is too thick, add a couple drops of milk.

3 Divide icing between two bowls, add 1 drop of blue food coloring to one bowl, and mix until blue

4 Drizzle white icing over the cooled cookies

5 Then drizzle on blue icing, so it looks messy and swirly

6 Let the icing dry and harden for 1 hour before eating the cookies

juicy jellies

PACKAGE OF GELATIN POWDER

1 Pick any juice (except for pineapple or kiwi)

2 Pour 2 cups of any fruit juice (or combine two flavors) in a measuring cup

3 Pour ½ cup into a small bowl and sprinkle on a package of gelatin

4 Pour another ½ cup juice into a small pot and bring to a boil on high heat

hot

5 When it boils, remove pot from the heat. Add the thick gelatin and juice paste. Whisk until paste dissolves.

6 Pour hot juice back into measuring cup

7 Pour liquid into whatever container you would like to make your jelly in

8 Cover with a lid or plastic wrap

9 Refrigerate the jelly for 2 hours or overnight

163

Add diced fresh fruit or whole berries.
DO NOT add pineapple, kiwi or ginger. They stop the jelly from firming up.
Just drink it and let it turn into jelly in your belly!
Hey, look, it works! I can finally be a jelly belly dancer!
jelly belly! oh yeah! jelly belly! I have a jelly dancer jelly belly!
oheksno!

A berried treasure map...

berried treasure crumble

1 Preheat oven to **375°F** 190°C

2 Combine in a large bowl, with a large spoon:

sharp

2 cups frozen strawberries

2 cups frozen raspberries

2 cups frozen blueberries

zest and juice of 1 lemon

1 cup icing sugar

3 In another large bowl, combine:

1 cup butter

1 cup flour

2 cups oatmeal

1 cup sugar

pinch of salt

4 Use your hands to mash and crumble all the butter until everything looks like pebbly gravel

5 Pour the fruit mixture into a large oven-safe casserole dish

6 Scatter little pieces of crumble on top of the fruit mixture

7 Place the casserole dish on a baking sheet to catch anything that may spill over

8 Bake for **45** minutes

hot

9 Remove from the oven and let it cool down for 30 minutes before serving

About the Author

Chef Pierre A. Lamielle is the award-winning cookbook author of *Alice Eats: A Wonderland Cookbook* and *Kitchen Scraps: A Humorous Illustrated Cookbook*. Both won "Best Illustrated Cookbook in the World" at the Gourmand Cookbook Awards.

He loves to teach cooking to all ages. He prefers cooking with friends but is not afraid of a little friendly culinary competition. He even competed on *Top Chef Canada* and *Chopped Canada*, which he won.

He is very excited for you to meet the amazing cast of characters in *The Munchy Munchy Cookbook for Kids* and to learn all about cooking and eating tasty food.

About Familius

Familius is a global trade publishing company that publishes books and other content to help families be happy. We believe that the family is the fundamental unit of society and that happy families are the foundation of a happy life. We recognize that every family looks different, and we passionately believe in helping all families find greater joy. To that end, we publish beautiful books that help families live our 9 Habits of Happy Family Life:

- Love Together
- Play Together
- Learn Together
- Work Together
- Talk Together
- Heal Together
- Read Together
- Eat Together
- Laugh Together

Website: www.familius.com
Facebook: www.facebook.com/paterfamilius
Twitter: @familiustalk, @paterfamilius1
Pinterest: www.pinterest.com/familius

The most important work you ever do will be within the walls of your own home.